# Chinese Characters List

| Writing | Recognizing | Radicals | Sound Indicators | Sub Total |
|---|---|---|---|---|
| 大中小上下人好子看不<br>见个天山的一十我手白<br>口门二三四五六八九女<br>七土目左右 | 在地学是出<br>头两们孩吧<br>力爸日父男<br>入耳田安戈 | 土女人口手<br>日子门目白<br>山父田力入<br>一二八十大<br>小戈 | 土子目山田<br>大力白门巴 | 26 in top 100<br>10: 101–200<br>6: 201–300<br>6: 301–500<br>6: 501–1000<br>1: 1001– |
| 18+8+3+3+3=35 | 8+2+3+3+3+1=20 | 22 | | 55 |

练习本 A
EXERCISE BOOK A

Activity Workbook
1
活动练习本

卢毓文 编著
Sarah Lu

SCHOOL: _____

CLASS: _____

NAME: _____

北京语言大学出版社
BEIJING LANGUAGE AND CULTURE
UNIVERSITY PRESS

(京)新登字 157 号

**图书在版编目(CIP)数据**

嘻哈说唱学汉语·1 活动练习本 / 卢毓文编著.
—北京：北京语言大学出版社，2006
ISBN 7-5619-1602-7

Ⅰ．嘻…  Ⅱ．卢…  Ⅲ．汉语-对外汉语教学-习题  Ⅳ．H195.4

中国版本图书馆 CIP 数据核字(2006)第 019545 号

| 书　　　名： | 嘻哈说唱学汉语·1 练习本 A：活动练习本 |
|---|---|
| 责任印制： | 汪学发 |

| 出版发行： | 北京语言大学出版社 |
|---|---|
| 社　　　址： | 北京市海淀区学院路 15 号　邮政编码：100083 |
| 网　　　址： | www.blcup.com |
| 电　　　话： | 发行部　82303650 / 3591 / 3651 |
| | 编辑部　82303395 |
| | 读者服务部　82303653 / 3908 |
| 印　　　刷： | 北京中科印刷有限公司 |
| 经　　　销： | 全国新华书店 |

| 版　　　次： | 2006 年 12 月第 1 版　　2006 年 12 月第 1 次印刷 |
|---|---|
| 开　　　本： | 889 毫米×1194 毫米　1/16　印张：3 |
| 字　　　数： | 44 千字　　印数：1－3000 册 |
| 书　　　号： | ISBN 7-5619-1602-7 / H·06029 |
| | 02800（练习本 A＋B） |

凡有印装质量问题，本社负责调换。电话：82303590

# 目 录
## CONTENTS

Chinese Characters List

致教师

Unit 1 .................................................................. 1

    Answering in Mandarin (Lessons 1 – 3)

Unit 2 .................................................................. 10

    Body Parts (Lessons 4 – 6)

Unit 3 .................................................................. 20

    Counting (Lessons 7 – 11)

Unit 4 .................................................................. 27

    Counting & Numbers (Lessons 12 – 16)

Unit 5 .................................................................. 33

    Directions, Exit & Entrance, Family & Greetings (Lessons 17 – 20)

Answer Key .................................................................. 39

Inset: Examples of Students' Work

# 致教师

  Hip Hop 译成"嘻哈"，其实就是"韵文"，意指儿歌、童谣、口诀、顺口溜、打油诗等所有押韵的说唱形式。采用韵文形式，可引起动机、增加趣味性、操练句型、帮助记忆等，是语言学习中非常重要的教学法。音乐旋律对脑部发展、记忆力、和注意力也都有显著的帮助。双语对照的韵文就更加好教易学，有趣实用。

  该教材既可作辅助教材，亦可作主教材使用。内容偏重生活题材及日常用语。词汇方面先教高频字词，以便于即学即用；单元主题按字母顺序编排，以利于联想查询。书中插图皆为作者精心设计，不但字中有画、画中有字，往往画中还有话，正适合做看图说话练习。

  练习册配备 A、B 两本。A 本为活动练习本，习题形式多样，与课文配套使用，能帮助学生操练重点、增加复习机会。B 本为加强汉字练习本，偏重讲授系统的汉字基础知识，并进行书写练习，既可以按部就班地识字写字，又可与口语教材并用。每课口语练习至一定熟练程度时再学汉字，学生就能驾轻就熟了。

  最后，希望各位使用该教材的老师们都能从实际出发，灵活应用学生日常生活中最常出现的素材，结合视觉与听觉同步协调发展，以嘻哈说唱提高学习动机、以图解汉字帮助学生克服汉字学习的畏难情绪，逐步提高汉语的学习能力。

作者

livingmandarin@yahoo.com

# Unit 1 — Answering in Mandarin
## Lesson 1 – 3

1. 连一连 (lián yī lián)

   Draw a line to match each action word to its picture. The first one has been done for you.

① listen ← A. tīng

B. shuō

 C. wǒ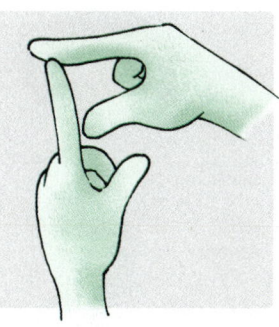

② me, I ⑤ Mandarin

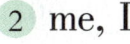 D. shénme

E. gēn

 F. pǔtōnghuà

 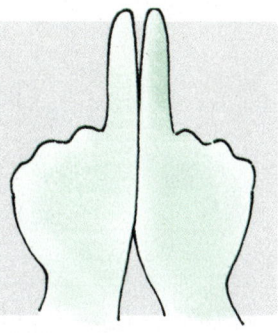

③ speak ⑥ with, follow

④ what

Chinese people tend to refer to themselves by pointing to their noses. Why?

1

## 2. 填一填 (tián yì tián)
Fill in the correct numbers to match each word to its picture.

1  you

2  speak

3  altogether

4  no, not

5  one person

A. bù　　　　＿＿＿＿＿

B. shuō　　　　__2__

C. nǐ　　　　＿＿＿＿＿

D. dàjiā yìqǐ　　　　＿＿＿＿＿

E. yí ge rén　　　　＿＿＿＿＿

3. 唱一唱 (chàng yí chàng)

Move to the beat.

### Pǔtōnghuà Pǔtōnghuà

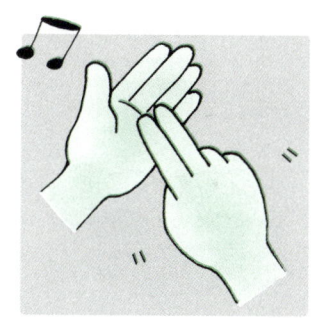

小 péngyǒu shuō

Pǔtōnghuà

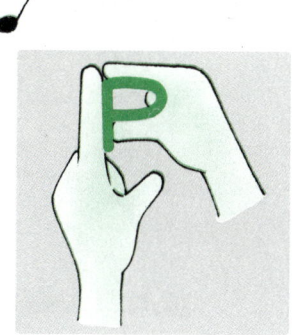

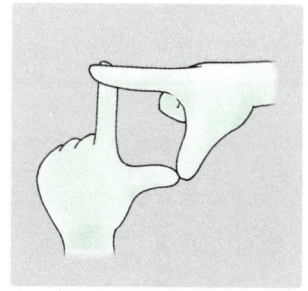

中 guózì 中 guózì

小 péngyǒu

xiě

中 guózì

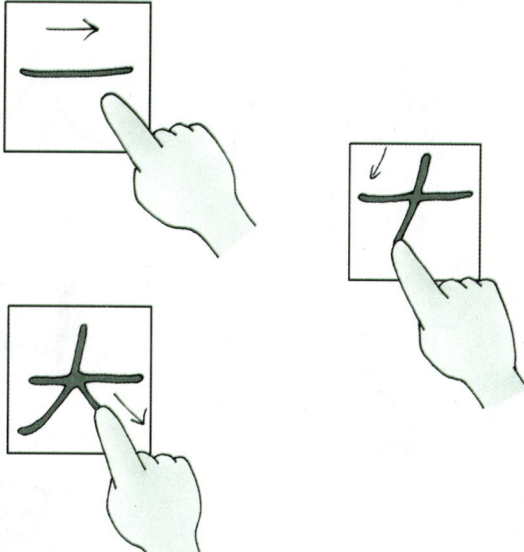

Please trace over each character with your index finger three times.

Unit 1: Lesson 1-3

3

Answering in Mandarin

## 4. 连一连 (lián yī lián)
Match the Chinese characters to their pictures, as in the example.

| | | |
|---|---|---|
| A | 1 大 | D (mouth) |
| B | 2 小 | E |
| C | 3 中 | F (ear) |
| | 4 人 | |
| | 5 口 | |
| | 6 耳 | |

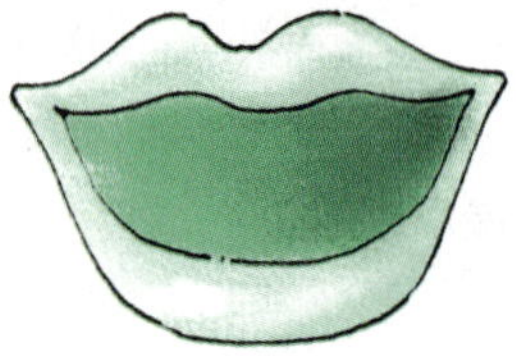

4

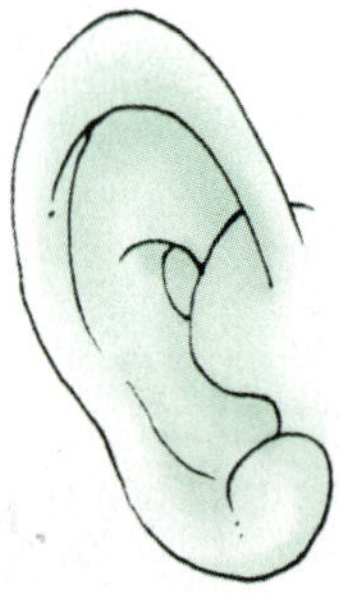

5 填一填 (tián yì tián)

Match the words to the pictures and write down the correct numbers in the brackets, as in the example.

tīng wǒ shuō ( 6 )

gēn wǒ shuō ( )

shénme ( )

bù shuō ( )

dàjiā ( )

yí ge rén ( )

xiě zì ( )

shuō huà ( )

6. 写一写、画一画(xiě yì xiě、huà yí huà)
   Writing Chinese Characters——横 héng

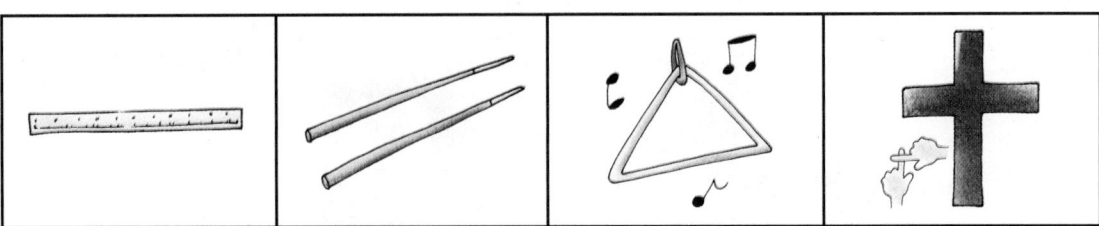

Trace over the characters and copy them underneath. In the last box, write the English word for the character and draw a picture to match the Chinese character.

## 7. 写一写、画一画 (xiě yi xiě、huà yí huà)
### Writing Chinese Characters —— 竖 shù  |

Trace over the characters and copy them underneath. In the last box, write the English word for the character and draw a picture to match the Chinese character.

Unit 1: Lesson 1–3

| 十 | 下 | 土 | 不 | 在 | 个 | 上 | 中 | 山 |

| 土 | 土 土 土 土 | |
| 在 | 在 在 在 在 | |
| 中 | 中 中 中 中 | |
| 上 | 上 上 上 上 | |

7

**Answering in Mandarin**

8. 填一填、练一练 (tián yí tián、liàn yí liàn)

Using Chinese characters, describe the size of the pictures below. Draw your own pictures that match the size.

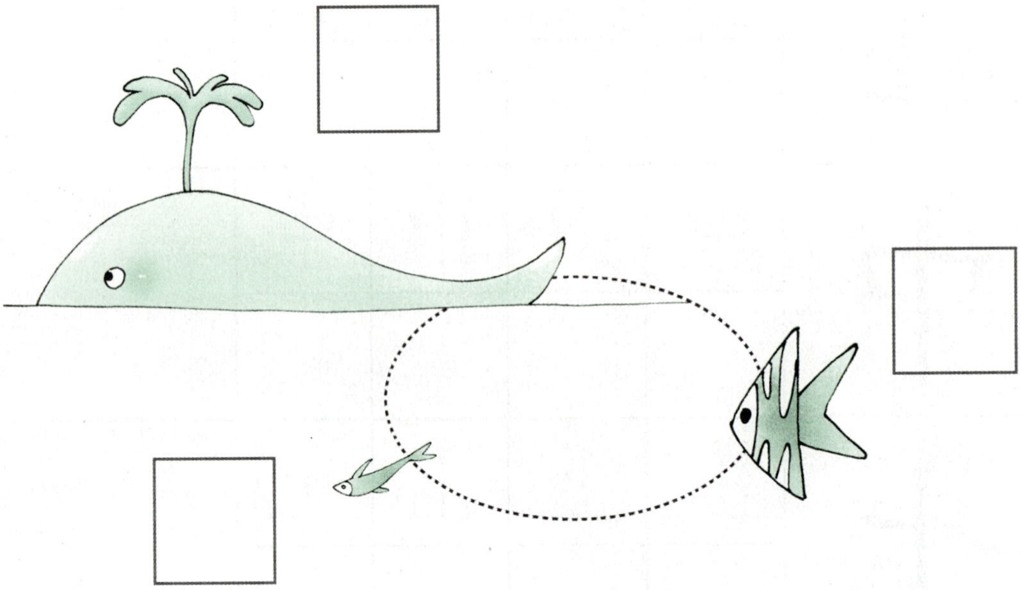

8

# CHARACTER SEARCH

Look for the characters that are the same. Colour the boxes with the same colour. Write the meaning of the character and how many similar characters you found.

| Characters | 口 | 人 | 耳 | 中 | 大 | 小 |
|---|---|---|---|---|---|---|
| Meaning | mouth | | | | | |
| Count the Character | 4 | | | | | |

| | | | | | |
|---|---|---|---|---|---|
| 大 | 口 | 人 | 小 | 人 | 大 |
| 耳 | 小 | 中 | 口 | 大 | 小 |
| 口 | 人 | 耳 | 中 | 耳 | 中 |
| 中 | 耳 | 大 | 人 | 大 | 小 |
| 人 | 大 | 口 | 大 | 小 | 人 |

Unit 1: Lesson 1–3

9

# Unit 2 — Body Parts
## Lesson 4 – 6

1. 连一连 (lián yì lián)
   Match the Chinese characters to their pictures.

1

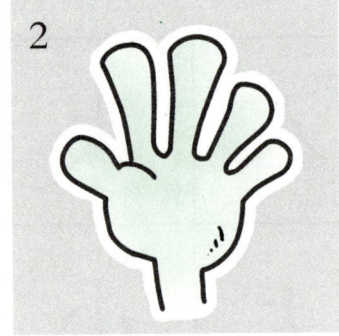
4

A 手
B 子
C 我
D 土
E 女
F 好

2

5

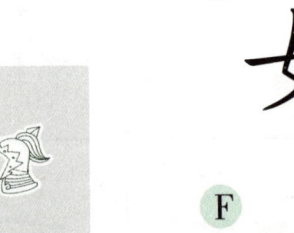
3

6

10

2. 连一连 (lián yí lián)
   Match the words to their pictures.

A head

B shoulders

C knees

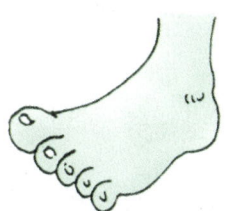
D foot

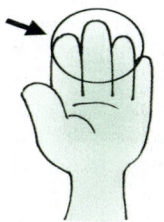
E fingers

1. tóu
2. shǒu
3. jiānbǎng
4. yǎnjing
5. xīgài
6. jiǎo
7. jiǎozhǐ
8. shǒuzhǐ
9. ěrduo
10. bízi
11. zuǐba

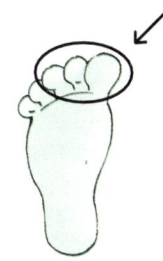
F toes

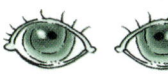
G eyes

H ears

I nose

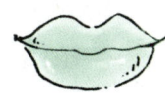
J mouth

K hand

Unit 2: Lesson 4–6

11

3. 玩一玩 (wán yì wán)
   Time to play.

4. 圈一圈 (quān yì quān)
   Circle the common parts these characters share.

| tǔ | zài |
|---|---|
| 土 | 在 |
| ground, earth | in, at |

| dà | tóu |
|---|---|
| 大 | 头 |
| big | head |

5. 找一找、填一填 (zhǎo yi zhǎo、tián yi tián)

Match the body parts with the Chinese words below. Write the correct word in the box. The first one has been done for you.

A. tóu
B.
C.
D.
E.
F.
G.
H.
I.
J.

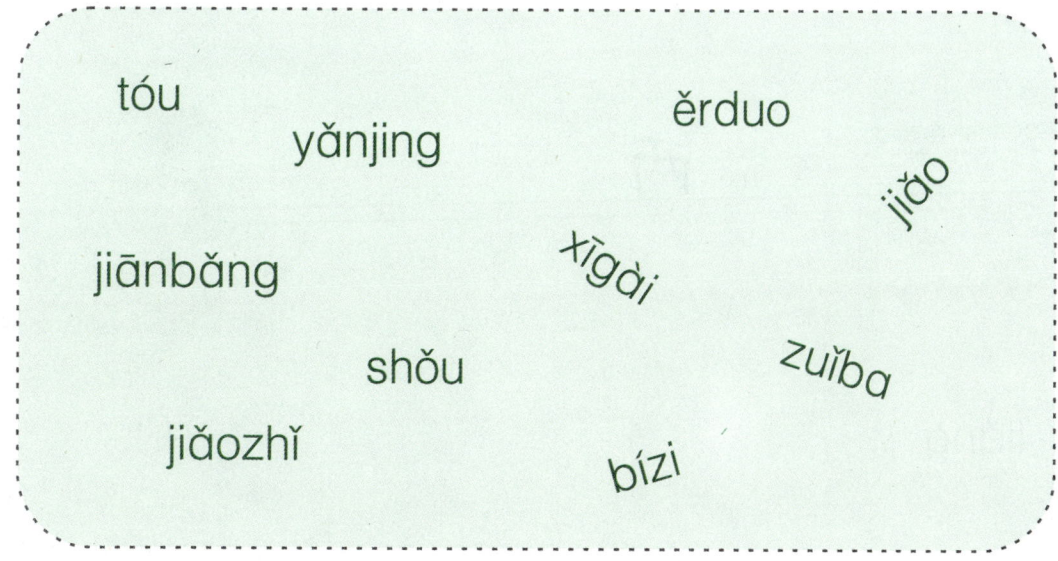

tóu  yǎnjing  ěrduo  jiǎo  jiānbǎng  xīgài  shǒu  zuǐba  jiǎozhǐ  bízi

Unit 2: Lesson 4–6

6. 填一填 (tián yì tián)
Match the Chinese characters to their pictures.

A hǎo

D dà

1 好 _____

2 不好 _____

3 大 _____

4 头 _____

B tóu

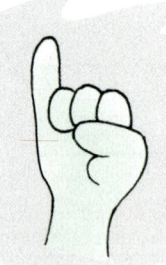

E bù hǎo

5 在 _____

6 两 _____

C liǎng

F zài

14

## 7. 写一写、画一画 (xiě yi xiě、huà yí huà)
Writing Chinese Characters — 点 diǎn

Trace over the characters and copy them underneath. In the last box, write the English word for the character and draw a picture to match the Chinese character.

Unit 2: Lesson 4-6

| 小 | 六 | 下 | 不 | 父 | 爸 | 我 | 的 | 安 |
|---|---|---|---|---|---|---|---|---|
| 六 | 六 | 六 | 六 | 六 | | | | |
| 下 | 下 | 下 | 下 | 下 | | | | |
| 不 | 不 | 不 | 不 | 不 | | | | |
| 小 | 小 | 小 | 小 | 小 | | | | |

15

8. 写一写、画一画（xiě yī xiě、huà yī huà）
   Writing Chinese Characters—撇 piě ノ 捺 nà ヽ

Trace over the characters and copy them underneath. In the last box, write the English word for the character and draw a picture to match the Chinese character.

| 人 | 大 | 八 | 天 | 不 | 在 | 父 | 个 | 手 |

16

# CHARACTER SEARCH

Look for the characters that are the same. Colour the boxes with the same colour. Write the meaning of the character and how many similar characters you found.

| Characters | 手 | 女 | 好 | 在 | 子 | 我 | 土 |
|---|---|---|---|---|---|---|---|
| Meaning | hand | | | | | | |
| Count the Character | 3 | | | | | | |

| | | | | | |
|---|---|---|---|---|---|
| 土 | 在 | 我 | 土 | 女 | 手 |
| 好 | 女 | 子 | 我 | 在 | 土 |
| 在 | 我 | 在 | 手 | 子 | 女 |
| 女 | 土 | 好 | 子 | 我 | 在 |
| 在 | 手 | 我 | 土 | 好 | 子 |

Unit 2: Lesson 4–6

17

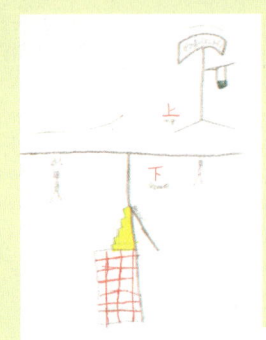

女男女

金木水火土

女人心口言

日月纟竹艹

手足疒虫辶

大中小

# Unit 3 — Counting
## Lesson 7 – 11

1. 选一选、读一读（xuǎn yī xuǎn、dú yī dú）
   Look and Talk. Match the correct phrase to the picture. Put a tick mark (√) in the bracket below the correct phrase, then read the phrase aloud.

   ① Shénme lái le?
      什么 来了？

   | 火车来了。<br>Huǒchē lái le.<br>(    ) | 娃娃 来了。<br>Wáwa lái le.<br>(    ) |
   |---|---|

   ② Shénme rén lái le?
      什么人　来了？

   | 两个小朋友<br>liǎng ge xiǎopéngyǒu<br>(    ) | 大家<br>dàjiā<br>(    ) | 他一个人<br>tā yí ge rén<br>(    ) |
   |---|---|---|

   ③ Yǒu jǐ ge rén?
      有 几个 人？

   | 三个人<br>sān ge rén<br>(    ) | 四个人<br>sì ge rén<br>(    ) | 八个人<br>bā ge rén<br>(    ) |
   |---|---|---|

   ④ Yǒu jǐ zhī?
      有 几只？

   | 三只<br>sān zhī<br>(    ) | 四只<br>sì zhī<br>(    ) | 两只<br>liǎng zhī<br>(    ) |
   |---|---|---|

20

## 2. 描一描声调 (miáo yì miáo shēngdiào)

Trace over the tone marks and read aloud.

| 1st tone  ˉ |   |   |
|---|---|---|
| 1 | 一 | yī |
| 3 | 三 | sān |
| (ear) | 听 | tīng |
| (mouth) | 说 | shuō |
| (hand) | 跟 | gēn |
| (top) | 中 | zhōng |
| he | 他 | tā |

| 4th tone  ˋ |   |   |
|---|---|---|
| 2 | 二 | èr |
| 4 | 四 | sì |
| (man) | 大 | dà |
| 字 | 字 | zì |
| look | 看 | kàn |
| up | 上 | shàng |
| down | 下 | xià |

## 3. 连一连 (lián yì lián)

Match the Chinese words to their English meanings. The first one has been done for you.

A. dàjiā
大家

B. tīng tā shuō
听他说

C. shuō huà
说话

D. yī èr yī
一二一

1. all
2. speak with him
3. say words
4. listen to him
5. don't speak
6. knees
7. must watch out
8. one two one

E. bù shuō
不说

F. gēn tā shuō
跟他说

G. xīgài
膝盖

H. yào zhùyì
要注意

21

4. 连一连 (lián yì lián)

Match the words to their pictures.

A

1  píngguǒ

2  xǐxǐ

B

3  gānjìng

4  bù gānjìng

D

C

5  shìzi

E

5. 填一填 (tián yì tián)

Fill in the blanks by writing the correct words for the family members.

A. bàba    B. gēge    C. jiějie

D. māma    E. dìdi    F. mèimei

22

6. 连一连 (lián yī lián)
Draw a line to match each Chinese character to its picture.

1 爸
2 上
3 下
4 目
5 看
6 四
7 山

7. 写一写、画一画（xiě yì xiě、huà yí huà）
   Writing Chinese Characters—勾 gōu

Trace over the characters and copy them underneath. In the last box, write the English word for the character and draw a picture to match the Chinese character.

Counting

| 小 | 子 | 家 | 好 | 丁 | 你 | 了 |

| 子 | 子 | 子 | 子 | 子 | |
| 女 | 女 | 女 | 女 | 女 | |
| 好 | 好 | 好 | 好 | 好 | |
| 丁 | 丁 | 丁 | 丁 | 丁 | |

24

8. 写一写、画一画（xiě yī xiě、huà yí huà）
   Writing Chinese Characters 一折 zhé

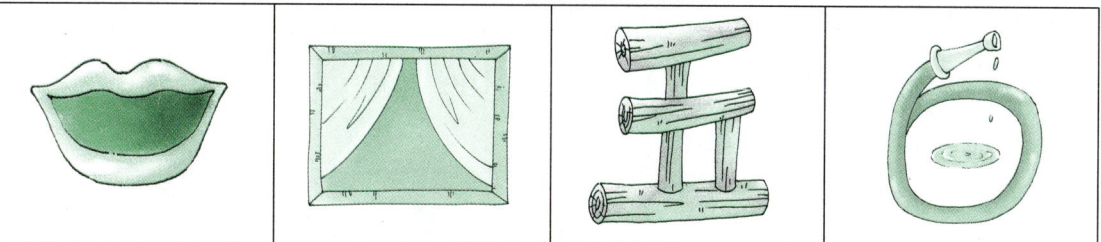

Trace over the characters and copy them underneath. In the last box, write the English word for the character and draw a picture to match the Chinese character.

Unit 3: Lesson 7-11

| 口 | 中 | 日 | 田 | 五 | 女 | 山 | 四 | 白 |

# CHARACTR SEARCH

Look for the characters that are the same. Colour the boxes with the same colour. Write the meaning of the character and how many similar characters you found.

| Characters | 上 | 下 | 不 | 看 | 见 | 四 | 孩 |
|---|---|---|---|---|---|---|---|
| Meaning | up | | | | | | |
| Count the Character | 3 | | | | | | |

| | | | | | |
|---|---|---|---|---|---|
| 上 | 下 | 四 | 不 | 孩 | 看 |
| 看 | 见 | 下 | 孩 | 看 | 下 |
| 四 | 孩 | 看 | 四 | 不 | 见 |
| 下 | 见 | 四 | 看 | 见 | 上 |
| 不 | 上 | 孩 | 下 | 孩 | 不 |

Counting

26

# Unit 4 — Counting and Numbers
## Lesson 12 – 16

1. 填一填 (tián yi tián)

   Can you fill in the missing numbers?

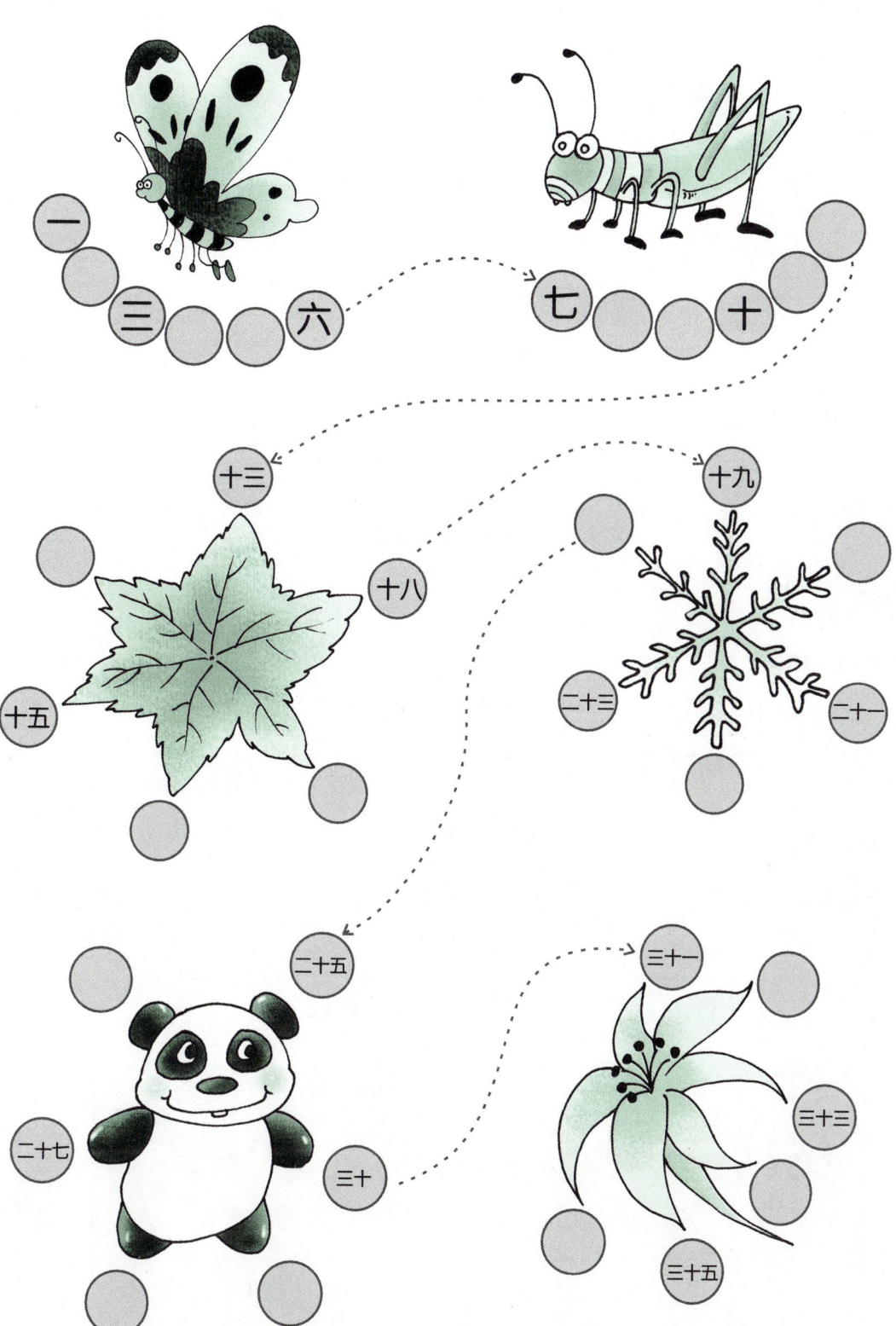

## 2. 玩一玩 (wán yi wán)

Time to play.

〇, 五 or 十?

NOTE:

| | | |
|---|---|---|
| 输 | shū | lose |
| 赢 | yíng | win |

| 2nd Tone ˊ | | 3nd Tone ˇ | |
|---|---|---|---|
| 十 | shí | 五 | wǔ |
| 零 (〇) | líng | | sōngshǔ |
| | méiyǒu | | lǎoshǔ |
| | yéye | | jiějie |

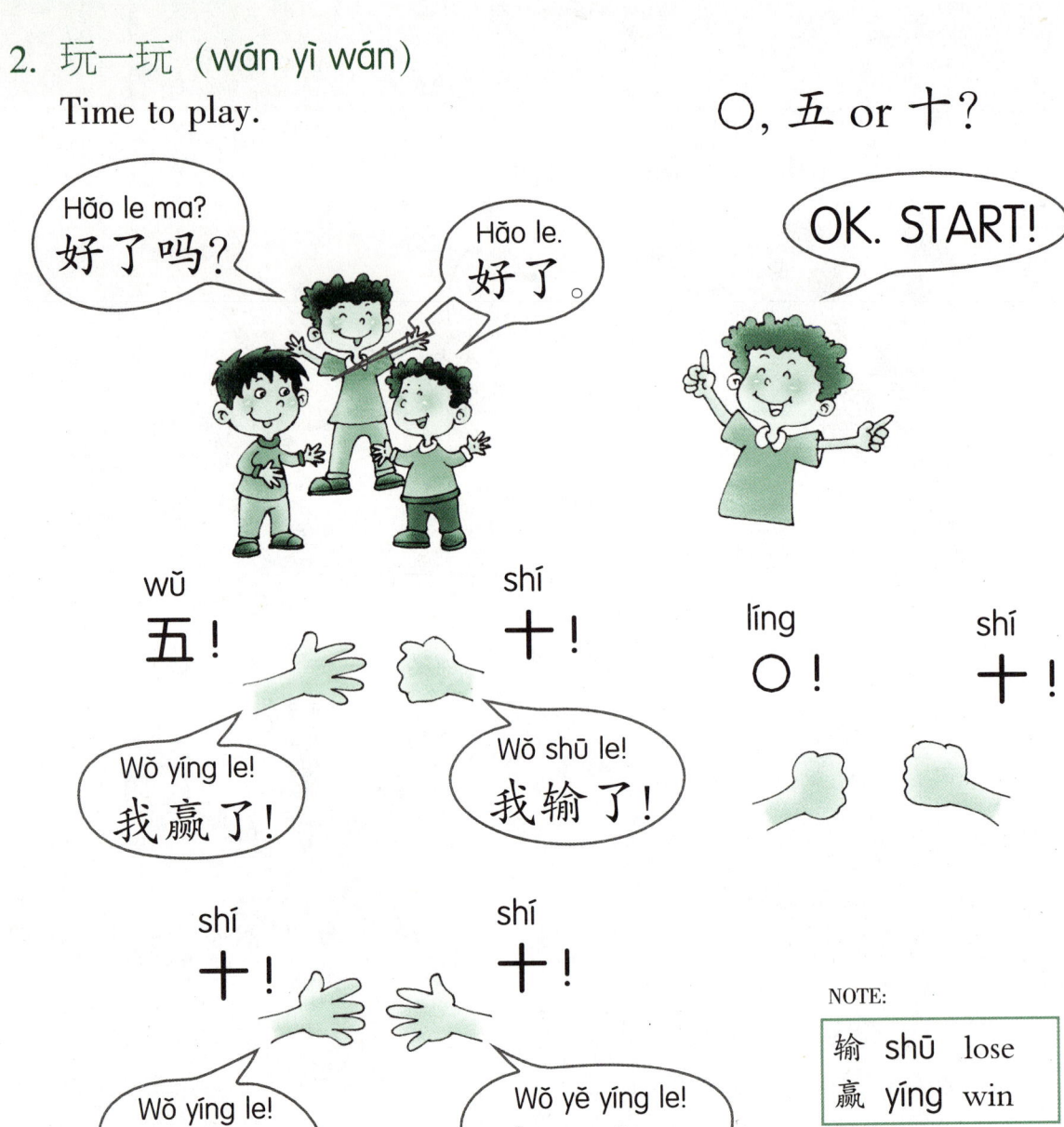

3. 写一写、画一画（xiě yī xiě、huà yī huà）
   Writing Chinese Characters — 勾 gōu

Trace over the characters and copy them underneath. In the last box, write the English word for the character and draw a picture to match the Chinese character.

Unit 4: Lesson 12–16

| 水 | 老 | 目 | 的 | 力 | 男 | 见 | 九 |

九 — 九 九 九 九

力 — 力 力 力 力

见 — 见 见 见 见

目 — 目 目 目 目

5. 写一写、画一画(xiě yī xiě、huà yí huà)
Writing Chinese Characters—提 ㇀   斜勾 xiégōu ㇂

Trace over the characters and copy them underneath. In the last box, write the English word for the character and draw a picture to match the Chinese character.

| 江 | 打 | 沙 | 戈 | 我 | 手 | 找 |
|---|---|---|---|---|---|---|
| 手 | 手 | 手 | 手 | 手 | | |
| 戈 | 戈 | 戈 | 戈 | 戈 | | |
| 我 | 我 | 我 | 我 | 我 | | |
| 打 | 打 | 打 | 打 | 打 | | |

Counting and Numbers

30

6. 连一连、猜一猜(lián yī lián、cāi yī cāi)

What is the picture? Join the numbered dots to find out and then colour it as you like.

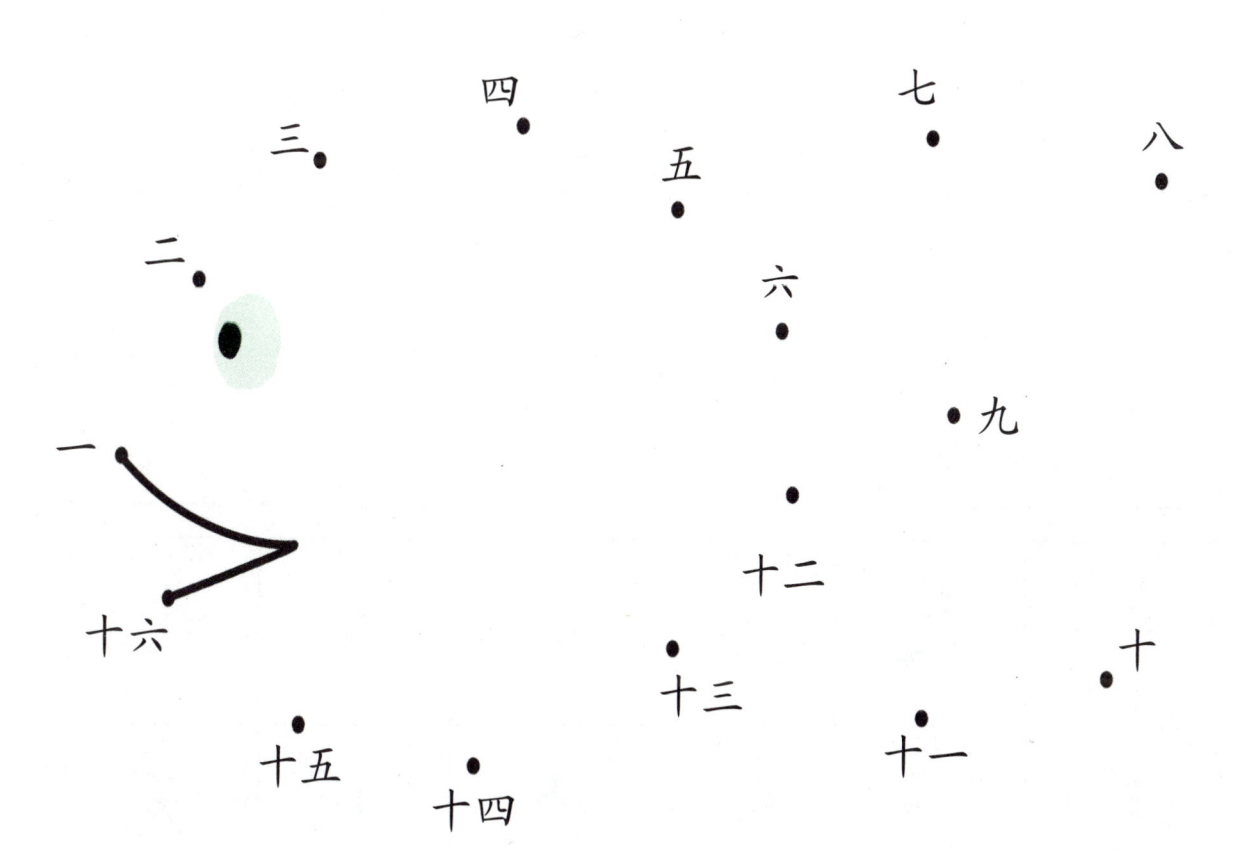

三 四 七 八
二 五
 六
 九
一 十二
 十
十六 十三
 十一
十五
 十四

Unit 4: Lesson 12–16

7. 写一写 (xiě yī xiě)

Write the Chinese characters for the numbers 9 to 15.

| 8 | 9 | 10 | 11 | 12 | 13 | 14 | 15 |
|---|---|----|----|----|----|----|----|
| 八 |   |    |    |    |    |    |    |

31

# CHARACTER SEARCH

Look for the characters that are the same. Colour the boxes with the same colour. Write the meaning of the character and how many similar characters you found.

| Characters | 八 | 男 | 天 | 七 | 爸 | 力 | 九 |
|---|---|---|---|---|---|---|---|
| Meaning | eight | | | | | | |
| Count the Character | 3 | | | | | | |

| | | | | | |
|---|---|---|---|---|---|
| 八 | 天 | 力 | 男 | 九 | 七 |
| 七 | 爸 | 天 | 九 | 七 | 天 |
| 力 | 九 | 男 | 八 | 天 | 爸 |
| 爸 | 天 | 七 | 九 | 爸 | 力 |
| 男 | 八 | 九 | 力 | 九 | 男 |

# Unit 5

**Directions, Exit and Entrance, Family and Greetings**

Lesson 17 – 20

1. 连一连（lián yī lián）
   Draw a line to match the Chinese characters to its picture.

出
入
门
们
和
山
左
右

## 2. 填一填 (tián yī tián)

Match the Chinese characters to their pictures.

H ( ) A ( )
G ( ) B ( )
F ( ) C ( )
E ( ) D ( )

8. 三 ge 女 háizi
3. 我看见 huǒchē 了。
5. 十和五是十五。
6. Qǐng nǐ chī.
4. 我和 péngyou chī shuǐguǒ.
1. xiě 中 guózì
2. Tīng!
7. Fēijī lái le!

34

3. 圈一圈（quān yì quàn）

Circle the letter below the picture that matches the Chinese character.

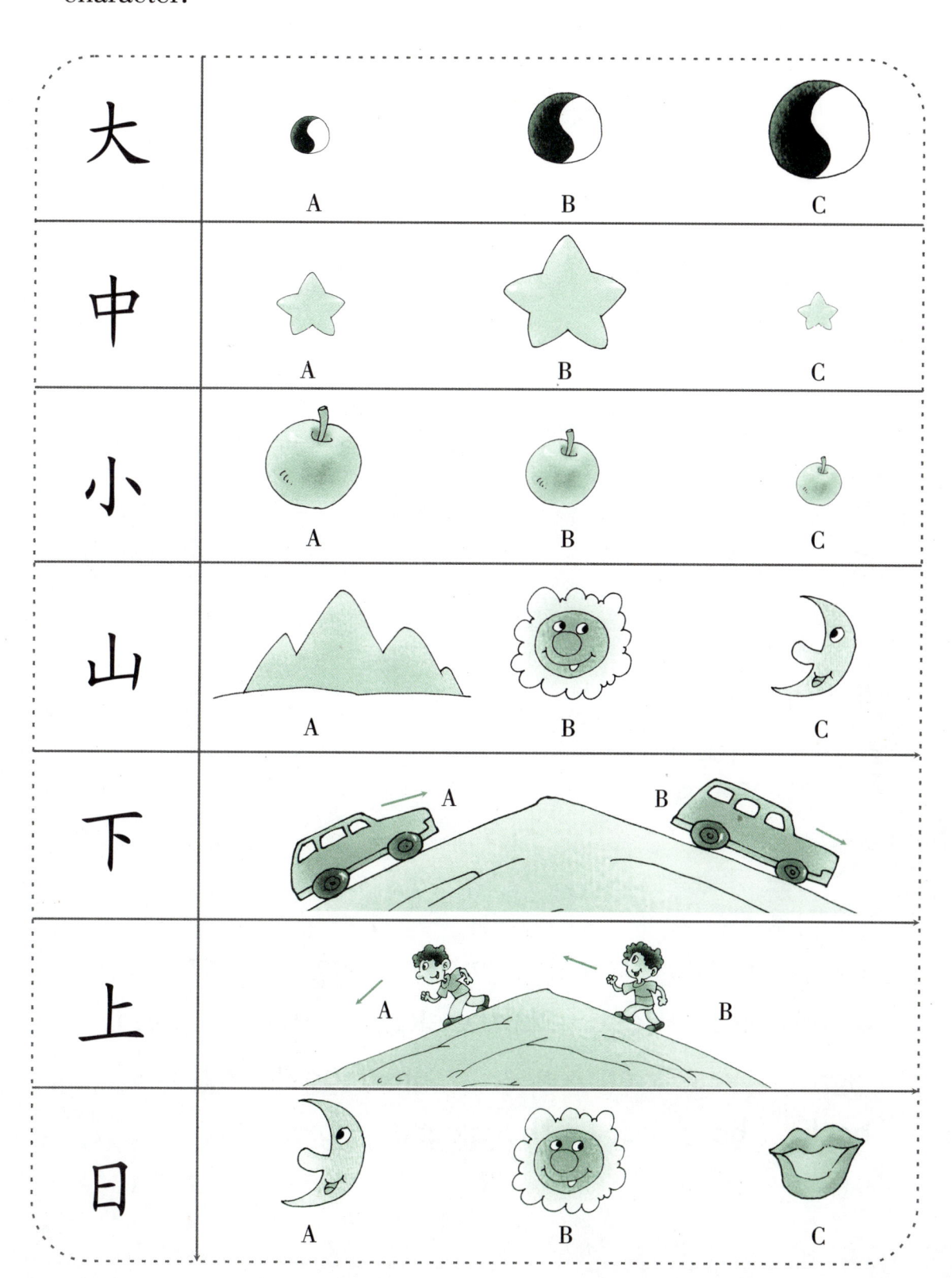

| 大 | A | B | C |
| 中 | A | B | C |
| 小 | A | B | C |
| 山 | A | B | C |
| 下 | A | B | |
| 上 | A | B | |
| 日 | A | B | C |

Unit 5: Lesson 17–20

35

## 4. 反义词 (fǎnyìcí)

What are the opposites? Match the opposite meaning and fill in the English words or phrases from the list below. The first one has been done for you.

1. 大 — big
2. 父 _____
3. 天上 _____
4. 左 _____
5. 上 lóu _____
6. qiánmiàn _____
7. 出口 _____
8. 不 _____
9. gōngjī _____
10. 男 hái 子 _____
11. 头 _____

A. _____ 子
B. _____ 下 lóu
C. _____ hòumiàn
D. small — 小
E. _____ mǔjī
F. _____ 脚
G. _____ 地下
H. _____ 女 hái 子
I. _____ 入口
J. _____ 是
K. _____ 右

exit, head, boy, rooster, no, front, go upstairs, left, in the sky, father, feet, right, yes, entrance, son, go downstairs, back, hen, down the ground, girl.

# CHARACTER SEARCH

Look for the characters that are the same. Colour the boxes with the same colour. Write the meaning of the character and how many similar characters you found.

| Characters | 山 | 日 | 是 | 左 | 右 | 出 | 入 |
|---|---|---|---|---|---|---|---|
| Meaning | mountain | | | | | | |
| Count the Character | 3 | | | | | | |

| | | | | | |
|---|---|---|---|---|---|
| 是 | 日 | 左 | 山 | 右 | 是 |
| 左 | 山 | 右 | 出 | 日 | 入 |
| 出 | 右 | 是 | 右 | 是 | 出 |
| 是 | 入 | 日 | 入 | 左 | 右 |
| 右 | 左 | 出 | 是 | 出 | 山 |

Unit 5: Lesson 17–20

# Topics of study A to G

**Complete and decorate the chart:**

Answering in Mandarin   Body Parts
Counting   Counting and Number
Driections, Exit and Eatrance, Family and Greetings

      A nswering in      M andarin

# ANSWER KEY

## Unit 1:

P1  1. 连一连   1. A  2. C  3. B  4. D  5. F  6. E

P2  2. 填一填   1. C  2. B  3. D  4. A  5. E

P4  4. 连一连   1. E  2. C  3. B  4. A  5. D  6. F

P5  5. 填一填   ( 6 ) ( 7 ) ( 5 ) ( 1 ) ( 3 ) ( 8 ) ( 2 ) ( 4 )

P9  CHARACTER SEARCH

| Characters | 口 | 人 | 耳 | 中 | 大 | 小 |
|---|---|---|---|---|---|---|
| Meaning | mouth | person | ear | middle | big | small |
| Count the Character | 4 | 6 | 4 | 4 | 7 | 5 |

## Unit 2:

P10  1. 连一连   1. D  2. A  3. C  4. F  5. B  6. E

P11  2. 连一连   1. A  2. K  3. B  4. G  5. C  6. D  7. F  8. E
                 9. H  10. I  11. J

P13  5. 找一找,填一填
    A. tóu  B. yǎnjing  C. xīgài  D. jiānbǎng  E. jiǎo
    F. jiǎozhǐ  G. zuǐba  H. shǒu  I. ěrduo  J. bízi

P14  6. 填一填   1. A  2. E  3. D  4. B  5. F  6. C

P17  CHARACTER SEARCH

| Characters | 手 | 女 | 好 | 在 | 子 | 我 | 土 |
|---|---|---|---|---|---|---|---|
| Meaning | hand | female | good | at, in, on | son, child | I, me | earth |
| Count the Character | 3 | 4 | 3 | 6 | 4 | 5 | 5 |

39

## Unit 3 :

P₁₈    1. 选一选,读一读    1.娃娃来了   2.大家   3.四个人   4.三只

P₁₉    3. 连一连      1. A   2. F   3. C   4. B   5. E   6. G   7. H   8. D

P₂₀    4. 连一连      1. A   2. B   3. D   4. E   5. C

        5. 填一填      1. A   2. D   3. B   4. E   5. C   6. F

P₂₁    6. 连一连      1. F   2. C   3. G   4. A   5. E   6. D   7. B

P₂₄    CHARACTER SEARCH

| Characters | 上 | 下 | 不 | 看 | 见 | 四 | 孩 |
|---|---|---|---|---|---|---|---|
| Meaning | up | down | no | watch, look, read | see | four | child |
| Count the Character | 3 | 5 | 4 | 5 | 4 | 4 | 5 |

## Unit 4 :

P₂₅    1. 填一填

P₂₉    6. 连一连,猜一猜    鱼

       7. 写一写

| 8 | 9 | 10 | 11 | 12 | 13 | 14 | 15 |
|---|---|---|---|---|---|---|---|
| 八 | 九 | 十 | 十一 | 十二 | 十三 | 十四 | 十五 |

P₃₀    CHARACTER SEARCH

| Characters | 八 | 男 | 天 | 七 | 爸 | 力 | 九 |
|---|---|---|---|---|---|---|---|
| Meaning | eight | male, boy | sky | seven | father, dad | power, strength | nine |
| Count the Character | 3 | 4 | 5 | 4 | 4 | 4 | 6 |

## Unit 5:

P31  1. 连一连  (1) 门  (2) 山  (3) 和  (4) 出  (5) 右  (6) 们  (7) 入  (8) 左

P32  2. 填一填  1. D  2. A  3. B  4. E  5. H  6. C  7. G  8. F

P33  3. 圈一圈  大—C  中—A  小—C  山—A  下—B  上—B  日—B

P34  4. 反义词

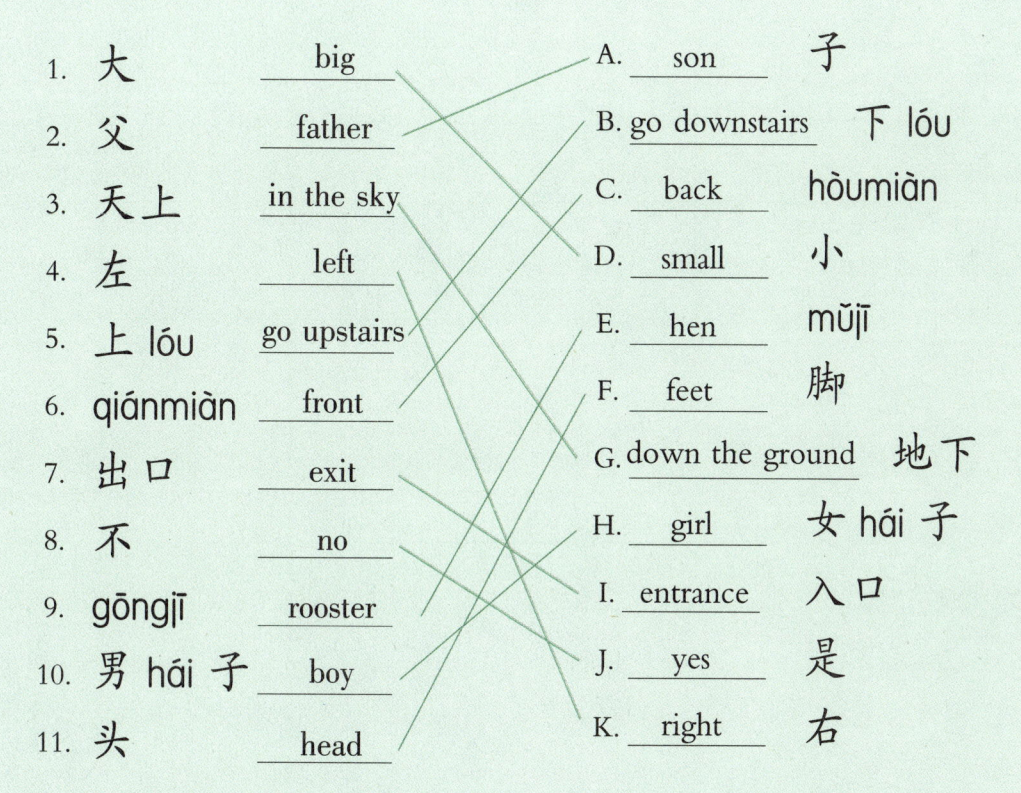

1. 大 — big
2. 父 — father
3. 天上 — in the sky
4. 左 — left
5. 上 lóu — go upstairs
6. qiánmiàn — front
7. 出口 — exit
8. 不 — no
9. gōngjī — rooster
10. 男 hái 子 — boy
11. 头 — head

A. son — 子
B. go downstairs — 下 lóu
C. back — hòumiàn
D. small — 小
E. hen — mǔjī
F. feet — 脚
G. down the ground — 地下
H. girl — 女 hái 子
I. entrance — 入口
J. yes — 是
K. right — 右

P35  CHARACTER SEARCH

| Characters | 山 | 日 | 是 | 左 | 右 | 出 | 入 |
|---|---|---|---|---|---|---|---|
| Meaning | mountain | sun, date | yes, is, are | left | right | out | in, enter |
| Count the Character | 3 | 3 | 6 | 4 | 6 | 5 | 3 |

41